G000128330

Mathstr Geometry

Creative tasks, activities and games for ages 11-14
Lesley Higgin

Angle Tangle

Work out all the missing angles in the rectangle.

(The diagram is not drawn to scale.)

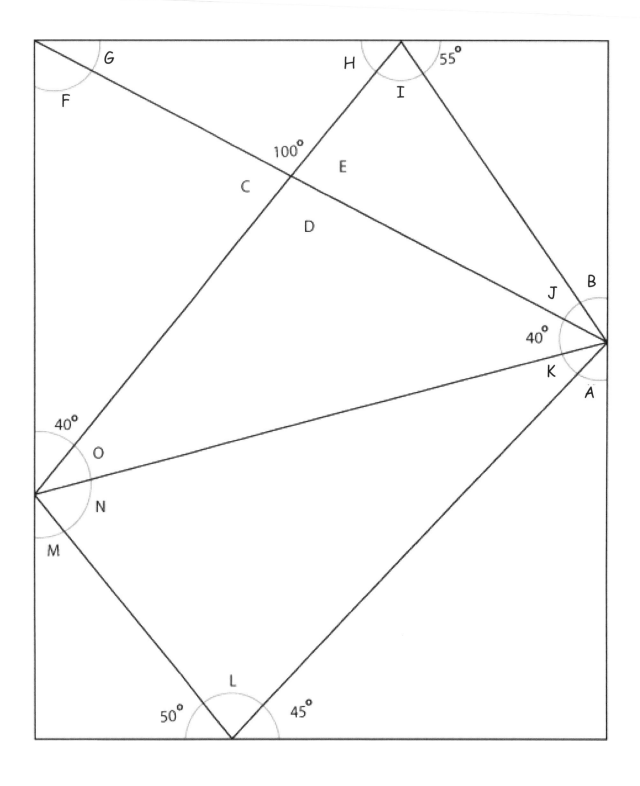

Angle Tangle 2

The following diagram is a rectangle which has been cut. The diagram is not drawn to scale.

Work out the lettered angles.

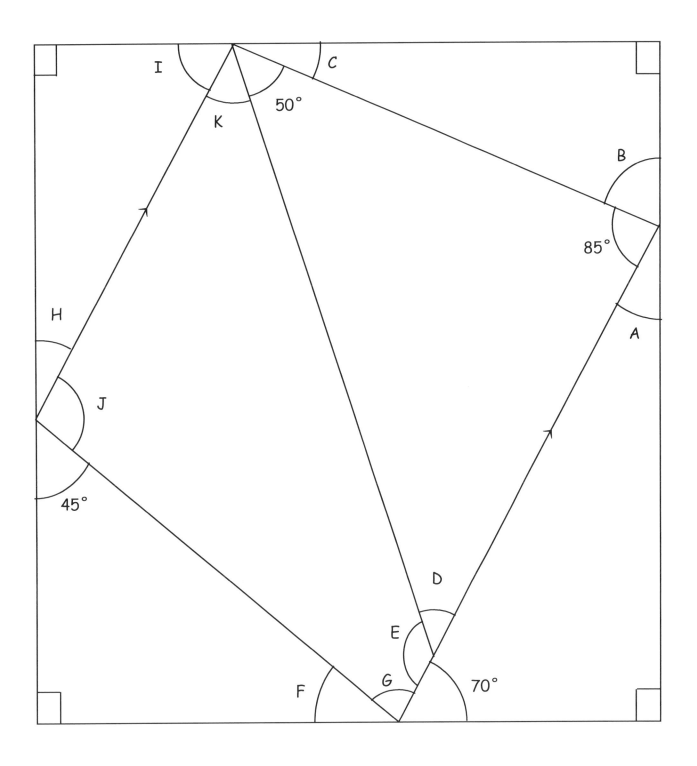

Properties of Quadrilaterals

Choose 1 quadrilateral to go with each definition.

There is only one way of doing it so that every definition has a quadrilateral.

PROPERTY	QUADRILATERAL
All angles are equal	....
All sides are equal	....
1 pair of parallel sides	....
4 lines of symmetry	....
Opposite sides are parallel	....
1 line of symmetry	....

QUADRILATERALS

Choose from:

Trapezium

Rhombus

Kite

Rectangle

Square

Parallelogram

Polygon Properties

Cut out the properties cards and place them in the grid so that the statements on either side of each polygon are correct.

square		rhombus		parallelogram
equilateral triangle				scalene triangle
rectangle		kite		isosceles triangle

regular	all sides equal	all angles equal	opposite sides parallel
2 pairs of equal sides	angles add to 180°	no lines of symmetry	one line of symmetry

Quad Squad

A. Work out the missing angles in each of the following quadrilaterals. A sketch of the quadrilateral will help you.

	Quadrilateral		Angles		
1.	parallelogram	36°	____	____	____
2.	square	____	____	____	____
3.	rhombus	121°	____	____	____
4.	trapezium	23°	62°	____	____
5.	kite	110°	22°	____	____

(There are two possible answers to question 5)

B. In the cases of the following two quadrilaterals, work out the missing angle and then state what type of quadrilateral it might be.

Sketch your answer, labelling each angle.

	Quadrilateral		Angles		
1.	_____	27°	153°	27°	____
2.	_____	90°	90°	140°	____

Bearing Codes

Start at the dot in the blank square and follow the instructions. At each change of direction, write down the letter of the cell you are in.
When you have finished, you should have the name of a mathematician.

Mathematician 1

- Travel 7cm on a bearing of 175°

- Travel 17 cm on a bearing of 340°

- Travel 12cm on a bearing of 100°

- Travel 12cm on a bearing of 260°

- Travel 5cm on a bearing of 020°

- Travel 7cm on a bearing of 140°

Mathematician 2

- Travel 5cm on a bearing of 240°

- Travel 7cm on a bearing of 170°

- Travel 17cm on a bearing of 355°

- Travel 13cm on a bearing 160°

- Travel 3cm on a bearing of 020°

- Travel 12cm on a bearing of 340°

- Travel 5.5cm on a bearing of 210°

- Travel 3cm on a bearing of 090°

- Travel 14cm on a bearing of 190°

Bearing Codes

A	J	R
B	K	S
C	L	T
D	M	U
E	•	V
F	N	W
G	O	X
H	P	Y
I	Q	Z

Measure for Treasure

The following map has been discovered on a remote island.

Follow the instructions to locate the position of the treasure on the map.

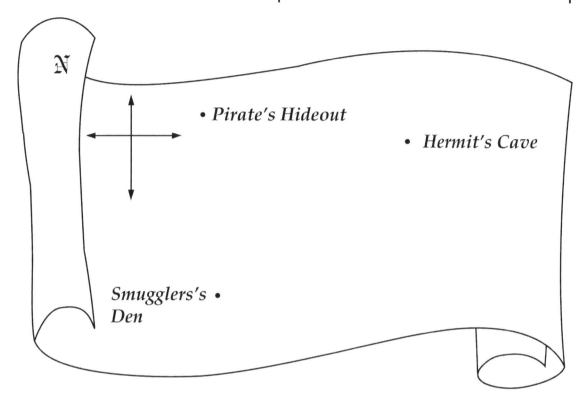

Instructions

There is a road connecting Pirate's Hideout with Hermit's Cave. Draw this.

There is a rough track which cuts the road in half at right angles. Draw this.

There is an underground tunnel which connects Pirate's Hideout and Smuggler's Den. Draw this on the map.

There is a dirt road which goes over the middle of the tunnel at right angles. Draw this on your map.

The treasure can be found at the point where the rough track and the dirt road meet.

Smallest to Largest

Put the following lengths in order starting with the smallest:

1	1 yard	4 feet	60 cm	30 inches	1 m
2	260mm	34cm	10 inches	1 foot	0.2 m
3	99 inches	4 yards	10 feet	2 m	340 cm
4	1100 m	1 mile	1 km	200000 cm	

Area Puzzle 1

The diagram shows a square of side 10cm.
The square has been cut up into different pieces.

Find the areas of the pieces marked A, B, C and D.

(Each line is an exact number of centimetres and the diagram
is not drawn to scale)

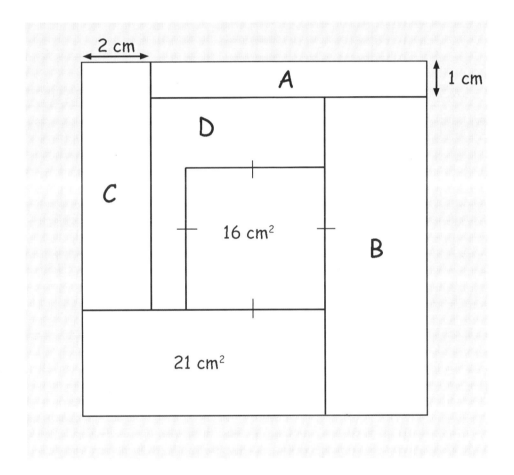

Area Puzzle 2

The diagram shows a square of side 12cm, which has been cut into smaller squares and rectangles.
The diagram is not drawn to scale.

Work out the lettered areas.

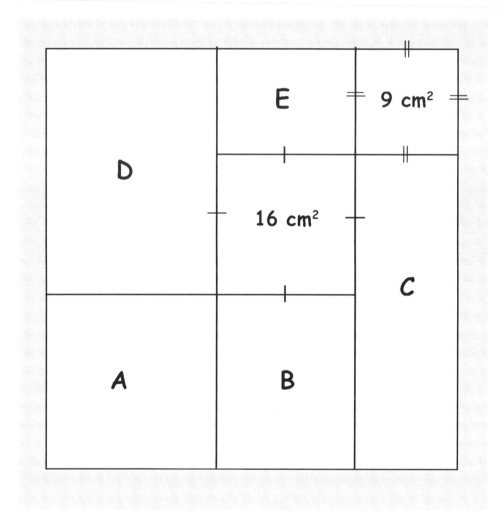

Area Puzzle 3

The following diagram is a 10cm × 10cm square, which has been cut into several triangles.

Work out the areas of the lettered triangles.

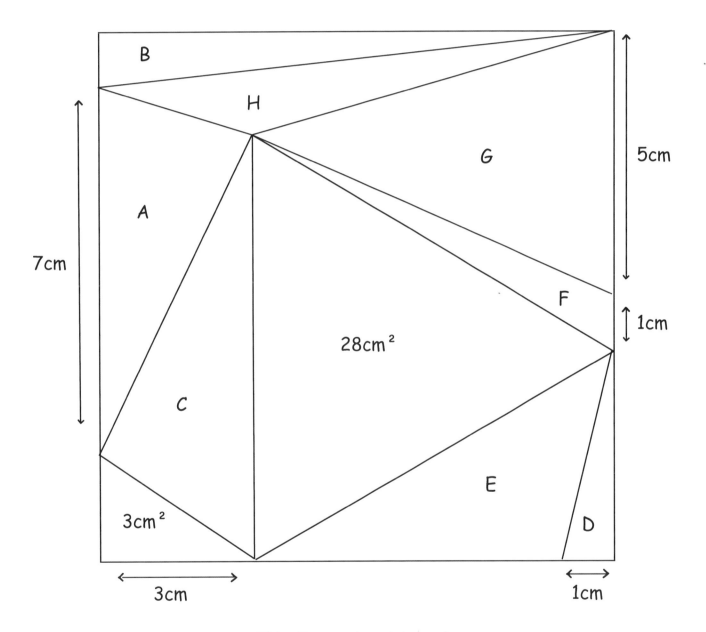

This diagram is not to scale.

Sticky Stack

'Sticky Stack' is a block of small pieces of paper, which are sticky on one side. They are used to make notes and reminders.

Each Sticky Stack has 500 pages. Each page measures 8cm × 8cm and is 0.1mm thick.

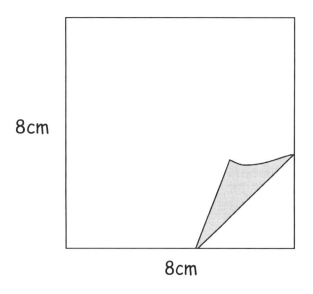

8cm

8cm

This is a top view of the Sticky Stack

A. Work out:

1. the height of a Sticky Stack

2. the volume of a Sticky Stack.

3. the total area of paper contained in a Sticky Stack.

B. Sticky Stacks are sold in packs of four.

1. Draw 4 different designs to show how the Sticky Stacks could be arranged in packs of four.

2. If you were employed to package the four Sticky Stacks in the most cost effective way, how would you do it?

Cubes and Cuboids

Fill in the gaps in the table below. A diagram may help.

	cube or cuboid	length	width	height	surface area	volume
1.		4cm	5cm	7cm		
2.		3cm	6cm			72cm^3
3.			1.5m	4m		15m^3
4.		2.4m		2m		24m^3
5.		4cm	4cm			64cm^3
6.		2cm	3cm		72cm^2	
7.	cube					216cm^3
8.		1cm		5cm	46cm^2	
9.		3.5m	4m	10m		
10.	cube				150m^2	

Find five different ways of completing the following table

11.						512m^3

- Try to find the cube or cuboid with volume 512cm^3, which has the smallest surface area.

Harry's House

Harry is making a scale model of his house. He is using a scale 1:200. Below is Harry's sketch of the net he will use to make his model. It is not drawn the scale.

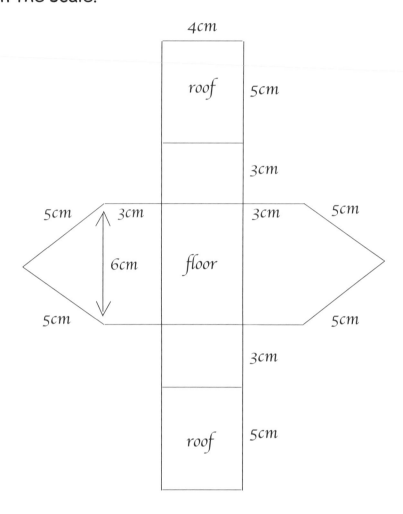

Draw the net accurately on card and make the model.
Use your model to help you to work out the following measurements of Harry's actual house.

1. the length and width

2. the floor area

3. the height

4. the angle between the two slanting sides of the roof

Prism Patterns

Imagine the following prisms:

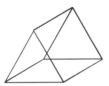 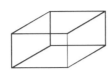

1. Name each prism.

2. For each prism, work out the number of sides the cross-section has. For example, the triangular prism has a cross-section of 3 sides.

3. Now work out the number of faces each prism has. Write your results in the following table:

Number of sides of cross-section (c)	3	4	5	6
Number of faces of prism (f)				

4. Find a rule connecting c and f.

5. Work out the number of vertices each prism has. Write your results in the following table:

Number of sides of cross-section (c)	3	4	5	6
Number of vertices of prism (v)				

6. Find a rule connecting c and v.

7. Work out the number of edges each prism has. Write your results in the following table:

Number of sides of cross-section (c)	3	4	5	6
Number of edges of prism (e)				

8. Find a rule connecting c and e.

9. Use your rules to predict how many faces, vertices and edges an octagonal prism will have. Check your prediction.

10. Try to explain **why** your rules work.

Money Makes the World Go Round

1.   Measure the diameter of a 1p coin in centimetres.

   a If you laid 1p coins side to side in a line, how many would you need to make a line 1 metre long?

   b How many would you need to make a line 1 kilometre long?

   c How many 1p coins would you need to stretch all the way around the Earth?

2. Measure the diameter of a 2p coin in centimetres.

   a How many 2p coins would make a line 1 metre long?

   b How many 2p coins would you need to stretch all the way around the Earth?

3. Measure the width of a 5p coin in millimetres.

   a If you laid 5p coins face to face, how many would you need to make a line 1 centimetre long?

   b How many would you need to make a line 1 metre long?

   c How many would you need to stretch around the Earth?

4. Use the following clues to work out the diameter of each of these foreign coins.

   Coin 1   1000 of these coins in a line would be 15 metres long.

   Coin 2   25 000 of these coins laid side to side would make a line 1 kilometre long.

   Coin 3   500 000 of these coins in a straight line would be 4 kilometres long.

Coordinates and Reflections

Draw a pair of axes with values from –8 to 8.

Plot the points for each shape.
Join those points connected with an arrow.

Shape

A.   (4, 1) → (3, 2) → (4, 3) → (5, 2) → (4, 1)

B.   (-5, -4) → (-3, -4)

C.   (3, 6) → (4, 5) → (5, 6)

D.   (4, -3) → (4, -5)

1.   Reflect shape A in the x-axis.

2.   Reflect shape B in the y-axis.

3.   Reflect shape C in the x-axis.

Make sure you label your diagrams so that they are clear,
showing the original shape and its reflection.

Coordinates and Transformations

1.   Draw a pair of axes with values from –8 to 8.

2.   Plot the points for each shape.

Join those points connected with an arrow.

Shape A   (–6, –2) ⟶ (–5, –1) ⟶ (–3, –1) ⟶ (–2, –2) ⟶ (–2, –6) ⟶
(–6, –6) ⟶ (–6, –2)

Shape B   (–7, 3) ⟶ (–7, 4) ⟶ (–6, 4) ⟶ (–6, 5) ⟶ (–2, 5) ⟶
(–2, 4) ⟶ (–1, 4) ⟶ (–1, 3) ⟶ (–7, 3)

Shape C   (3, –4) ⟶ (5, –4) ⟶ (4, -5) ⟶ (3, –4)

Shape D   (6, –1) ⟶ (6, –2) ⟶ (8, –2) ⟶ (8, –1)

3.   Reflect Shape C in the x-axis.

4.   Translate Shape B, 8 units to the right and 3 units up.

5.   Translate Shape D, 3 units to the left and 4 units up.

6.   Rotate Shape A 180° about the origin.

Two Transformations

Rotation 90° anti-clockwise centre (0,0)	Translation 2 units left	Reflection in the y-axis

Translation 4 units up	Reflection in x-axis

Choose two of the above transformations to move the shaded triangle to each of the lettered positions on the axes.

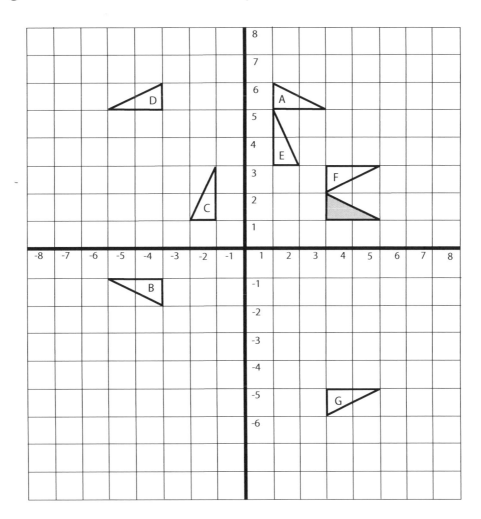

Teacher's Notes and Answers

Angle Tangle

Notes

This activity can be used as a class exercise by putting the diagram on a whiteboard or as indiviudal or pair work.

Pupils should be encouraged to explain how they decided on thier answers.

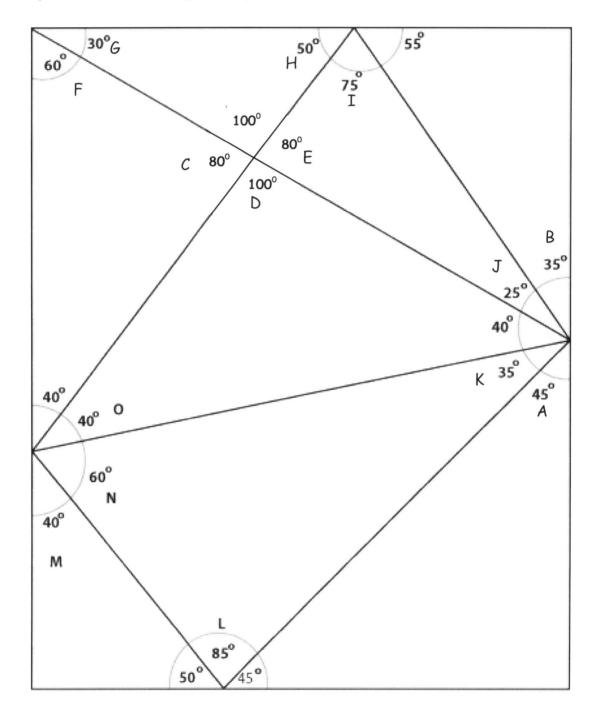

Angle Tangle 2

Notes

Pupils will require knowledge of angles in triangles, quadrilaterals and parallel lines to solve this puzzle.

The puzzle does not have to be solved in the order of the letters.

Answers

A	20°		G	65°
B	75°		H	20°
C	15°		I	70°
D	45°		J	115°
E	135°		K	45°
F	45°			

Properties of Quadrilaterals

Answers

PROPERTY	QUADRILATERAL
All angles are equal	rectangle
All sides are equal	rhombus
1 pair of parallel sides	trapezium
4 lines of symmetry	square
Opposite sides are parallel	parallelogram
1 line of symmetry	kite

Teaching Notes
Polygon Properties

Notes

This activity can either be used on the grid or can be used on a blank grid with a set of polygon cards and a set of properties cards (opposite), which is obviously more difficult.

Answers

square	all sides equal	rhombus	opposite sides parallel	parallelogram
regular				no lines of symmetry
equilateral triangle				scalene triangle
all angles equal				angles add to 180°
rectangle	2 pairs of equal sides	kite	one line of symmetry	isosceles triangle

square	rhombus		regular	all sides equal
scalene triangle	equilateral triangle		2 pairs of equal sides	angles add to 180°

parallelogram	kite		all angles equal	opposite sides parallel
rectangle	isoceles triangle		no lines of symmetry	one line of symmetry

Quad Squad

Notes

This activity lends itself to group work and class discussion, especially in part B where there are several possible answers. Pupils should be encouraged to make rough sketches.

Answers

A. Pupils may have written their angles in a different order

	Quadrilateral		Angles		
1.	parallelogram	36°	144°	36°	144°
2.	square	90°	90°	90°	90°
3.	rhombus	121°	59°	121°	59°
4.	trapezium	23°	62°	157°	118°
5.	kite	110°	22°	110°	118°
5.	or, kite	110°	22°	114°	114°

B.

1. The missing angle is 153°. The quadrilateral could be a parallelogram, a rhombus or an isosceles trapezium.

2. The missing angle is 40°. The quadrilateral could be a trapezium or a kite.

Bearing Codes

Notes

Having found the names of both mathematicians (notes on each mathematician included below), pupils could write their own names in code, to be checked by their friends.

Answers

Mathematician 1 is Pascal and mathematician 2 is Fibonacci.
Notes on each mathematician are given below.

Pascal

Blaise Pascal is remembered for 'Pascal's Triangle':

```
                1
            1       1
        1       2       1
    1       3       3       1
1       4       6       4       1
```

Pupils could be asked to work out the next few lines and the sums of each line.

Fibonacci

Fibonacci was the nickname of Leonardo Pisano. He is remembered for the 'Fibonacci Sequence'; 1, 1, 2, 3, 5, 8, 13, 21, ...

Pupils could be asked to work out the next few terms.
The Fibonacci sequence appears in nature. For example, a flower always has a number of petals which is a Fibonacci number.

Measure for Treasure

Notes

This activity practises drawing perpendicular bisectors.
A useful extension activity is for pupils to make up their own maps and instructions.
Pupils could include finding angle bisectors and midpoints in their instructions.

Answer

Pupils should draw the perpendicular bisector of Pirate's Hideout and Hermit's Cave and the perpendicular bisector of Pirate's Hideout and Smuggler's Den.

The treasure is where these cross.

Smallest to Largest

Notes

This activity practises conversions between metric and imperial measurements of length. Rough equivalents are sufficient.

Answers

1. 60 cm, 30 inches, 1 yard, 1 metre, 4 feet

2. 0.2 m, 10 inches, 260 mm, 1 foot, 34 cm

3. 2 m, 99 inches, 10 feet, 340 cm, 4 yards

4. 1 km, 1100 m, 1 mile, 200000 cm

Area Puzzle 1

Notes
The pupils must calculate that the rectangle of area 21cm², must be 3cm by 7cm.

Area D can be calculated by working out the lengths of its sides or by subtracting all the other areas from 100cm².

Answers

Area A = 8cm²   Area B = 27cm²

Area C = 14cm²   Area D = 14cm²

Area Puzzle 2

Notes
In addition to practising area, this activity can also be used to introduce the idea of a square root when calculating the sides of the two squares.

Answers

Area A = 25cm²   Area B = 20cm²

Area C = 27cm²   Area D = 35cm²

Area E = 12cm²

Area Puzzle 3

Notes
Pupils must work out the areas of the triangles in alphabetical order.
The only way to calculate the area of triangle H is to subtract the areas of all the other triangles from 100 cm².

Answers

Area A = 10.5 cm²   Area B = 5 cm²   Area C = 12 cm²

Area D = 2 cm²   Area E = 12 cm²   Area F = 3.5 cm²

Area G = 17.5 cm²   Area H = 6.5 cm²

Sticky Stack

Answers

A

1. 5 cm   2. 320 cm^3 3. 32 000 cm^2

B

1. There are 4 possible designs (not to scale) :

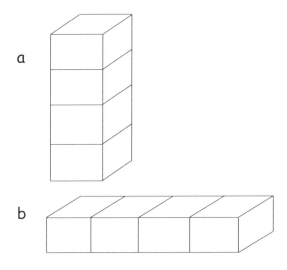
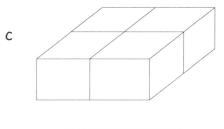

2. The most cost effective design should have the smallest surface area, as this means it will require less packaging material.

   The surface areas of the 4 different designs are:

   a) 768 cm^2 b) 912cm^2 c) 832cm^2 d) 736cm^2

   So, the most cost effective design is d.

Cubes and Cuboids

Answers

	cube or cuboid	length	width	height	surface area	volume
1.	cuboid	4cm	5cm	7cm	166cm²	140cm³
2.	cuboid	3cm	6cm	4cm	108cm²	72cm³
3.	cuboid	2.5m	1.5m	4m	39.5m²	15m³
4.	cuboid	2.4m	5m	2m	53.6m²	24m³
5.	cube	4cm	4cm	4cm	96cm²	64cm³
6.	cuboid	2cm	3cm	6cm	72cm²	36cm³
7.	cube	6cm	6cm	6cm	216cm²	216cm³
8.	cuboid	1cm	3cm	5cm	46cm²	15cm³
9.	cuboid	3.5m	4m	10m	178m²	140m³
10.	cube	5m	5m	5m	150m²	125m³

There are many different ways of completing the table in question 11.

The smallest surface area can be found in the following case:

11.	cube	8m	8m	8m	384m²	512m³

Harry's House

Notes

This activity practises both accurate drawing and working with scales.
If pupils are using glue to stick sides together, they will need to add tabs to their net before they cut it out.

Answers

1. 12m x 8m
2. $96m^2$
3. 14m
4. 74° (to nearest degree) (This question reinforces the fact that angles do not change under enlargement)

Prism Patterns

Notes

This provides a valuable opportunity for pupils to begin to explain and justify their results.

More able pupils could extend the ideas to pyramids.
(Formulae would be based on the shape of the base)

Answers

1. triangular prism, cuboid, pentagonal prism, hexagonal prism

2. 3, 4, 5, 6 sides respectively.

3.
Number of sides of cross-section (c)	3	4	5	6
Number of faces of prism (f)	5	6	7	8

4. $f = c + 2$

5.
Number of sides of cross-section (c)	3	4	5	6
Number of vertices of prism (v)	6	8	10	12

6. $v = 2c$

7.
Number of sides of cross-section (c)	3	4	5	6
Number of edges of prism (e)	9	12	15	18

8. $e = 3c$

9. An octagonal prism will have 10 faces, 16 vertices and 24 edges.

10. $f = c + 2$: Each prism has c faces perpendicular to the crosssection and another 2 faces which are the front and back of the prism.

   $v = 2c$: Each prism has c vertices on front and c vertices on back.

   $e = 3c$: Each prism has c edges on front, c edges on back and c edges joining front and back cross-sections.

Money Makes the World Go Round

Notes

Pupils will need to use the fact that the distance around the Earth is 40820km. However, the value 40 000km has been used in the following answers.

This means that a calculator is not needed for the worksheet and therefore the pupils will not run into the problem of notation in standard form.

This worksheet also offers useful revision of multiplication and division by multiples of 10, 100, 1000 ......

Answers

1. The diameter of a 1p coin is 2cm.

      a 50

      b 50 000

      c 2000 000 000

2. The diameter of a 2p coin is 2.5cm.

      a 40

      b 1 600 000 000

3. The width of a 5p coin is 1mm.

      a 10

      b 1000

      c 40 000 000 000

4. Coin 1 has diameter 1.5cm

    Coin 2 has diameter 4cm

    Coin 3 has diameter 8mm

Coordinates and Reflections

Answers

When the worksheet has been finished the pupils should have a stick man drawn in the 4th quadrant.

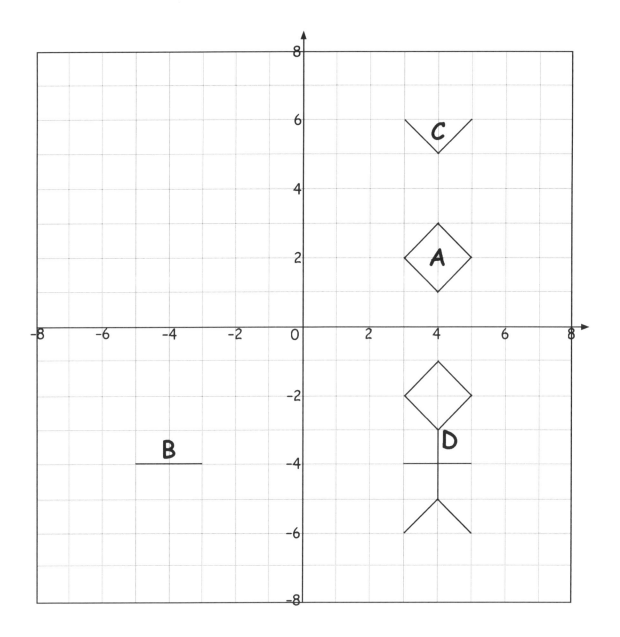

Coordinates and Transformations

Answers

The pupils should end up with a face (wearing a hat) in the 1st quadrant.
Nose and mouth are shown, but pupils should draw in the eyes themselves.

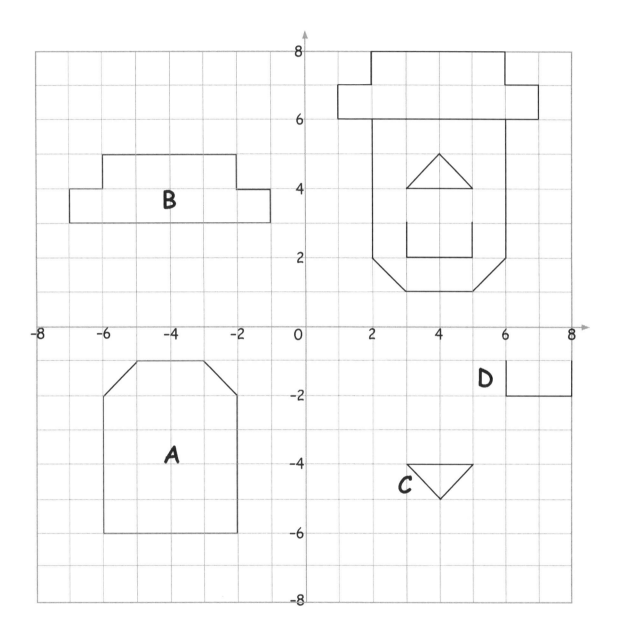

Two Transformations

Notes

When the activity has been completed, students could be asked to find out whether the order of the transformations make a difference.

A good extension activity is to ask pupils to find as many different positions of triangles as they can by doing two of the transformations.

Answers

Triangle	1st Transformation	2nd Transformation	Order Matters?
A	Translation 2 left	Translation 4 up	no
B	Reflection in x-axis	Reflection in y-axis	no
C	Translation 2 left	Rotation 90°	yes
D	Translation 4 units up	Reflection in y-axis	no
E	Rotation 90°	Reflection in y-axis	yes
or E	Reflection in x-axis	Rotation 90°	yes
F	Reflection in x-axis	Translation 4 up	yes
G	Translation 4 up	Reflection in x-axis	yes